Brands We Know

ESPN

By Sara Green

Bellwether Media • Minneapolis, MN

Jump into the cockpit and take flight with Pilot books. Your journey will take you on high-energy adventures as you learn about all that is wild, weird, fascinating, and fun!

This edition first published in 2018 by Bellwether Media, Inc.

Library of Congress Cataloging-in-Publication Data

Names: Green, Sara, 1964- author.
Title: ESPN / by Sara Green.
Description: Minneapolis, MN : Bellwether Media, Inc., 2018. | Series:
   Pilot: Brands We Know | Includes bibliographical references and index.
   Audience: Grade 3-8.
Identifiers: LCCN 2016052726 (print) | LCCN 2017021230 (ebook) |
   ISBN 9781626176515 (hardcover : alk. paper) | ISBN 9781681033815
   (ebook)
Subjects: LCSH: ESPN (Television network)--History--Juvenile
   literature. |Television broadcasting of sports--History--Juvenile
   literature.
Classification: LCC GV742.3 (ebook) | LCC GV742.3 .G74 2017 (print)
   | DDC 070.4497960973--dc23
LC record available at https://lccn.loc.gov/2016052726

Editor: Betsy Rathburn   Designer: Josh Brink

Printed in the United States of America, North Mankato, MN.

Table of Contents

What Is ESPN?

It is game day! A group of sports fans tunes in to ESPN to watch a football game. If the friends miss an important play, they can catch all the highlights on *SportsCenter*. This show offers news on football, basketball, and other favorite sports. Sports fans count on ESPN to keep them up-to-date!

ESPN, Inc. is an American sports entertainment company. Its **headquarters** is in Bristol, Connecticut. ESPN is one of the most popular cable **networks** in the world. Millions of people listen to ESPN radio stations every day. Its **apps** help fans stay connected to sporting events. ESPN publishes a sports magazine called *ESPN The Magazine*. It has won many awards. The company also owns a large sports **complex** in Florida. People all over the world recognize the ESPN **logo**. Today, the ESPN **brand** is worth nearly $17 billion!

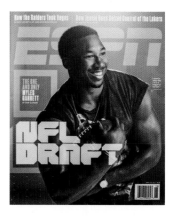

ESPN The Magazine

By the Numbers

more than
32
ESPN television
networks

about
8,000
ESPN employees

more than
64,000
hours of programs
produced
in 2016

20 million
ESPN Radio listeners
each week

64 million
visitors to ESPN.com
every month

16.5 million
readers per issue of
ESPN The Magazine

ESPN headquarters in Bristol, Connecticut

ESPN Kicks Off

Bill Rasmussen and his son, Scott, started ESPN in 1978. Bill was a former sports announcer. He thought television news spent too little time on sports. He wanted to find a way to bring more television sports to fans. Bill and Scott realized that **satellite** technology was the answer. It could be used to air sports on cable television. The men decided to use satellites from a company called RCA.

However, the satellites cost about $35,000 a month. Bill and Scott needed money to pay for them. Bill began asking companies to put money into ESPN. But many doubted that ESPN would work. Most companies turned the men down. Finally, an **advertiser** gave money. Then, the **NCAA** agreed to provide programs to the network. This led a company called Getty Oil to take a risk. It gave $10 million to the company. ESPN was up and running!

....

Naming A Network
ESPN was first called ESP Network. The name changed to ESPN in 1979. It is short for Entertainment and Sports Programming network.

The Radio Corporation of America Tells

What TELEVISION will mean to you!

On April 30th RCA television was introduced in the New York metropolitan area. Television programs, broadcast from the lofty NBC mast at the top of the Empire State Building, cover an area approximately fifty miles in all directions from that building. Programs from NBC television studios are sent out initially for an hour at a time, twice a week. In addition, there will be pick-ups of news events, sporting events, interviews with visiting celebrities and other programs of wide interest.

How Television will be received!

To provide for the reception of television programs, RCA Laboratories have developed several receiving sets which are now ready for sale. These instruments, built by RCA Victor, include three models for reception of television pictures and sound, as well as regular radio programs. There is also an attachment for present radio sets. This latter provides for seeing television pictures, while the sound is heard through the radio itself. The pictures seen on these various models will differ only in size.

Television—A new opportunity for dealers and service men

RCA believes that as television grows it will offer dealers and service men an ever expanding opportunity for profits. Those, who are in a position to cash in on its present development, will find that television goes hand in hand with the radio business of today.

In Radio and Television—It's RCA All the Way

RCA *Radio Corporation of America*
RADIO CITY, NEW YORK

**SPORTS
JUNKIES
REJOICE**

THE BIRTH OF
ESPN

BILL
RASMUSSEN

Bill Rasmussen

ESPN began **broadcasting** across the United States on September 7, 1979. Its first televised sporting event was a slow-pitch softball game. A sports news program called *SportsCenter* also aired for the first time that day. Around 30,000 people watched it. ESPN began airing a show called *Auto Racing* in 1979. The show later became *SpeedWorld*. It aired car and motorcycle races for nearly 30 years.

All Day Every Day
ESPN first aired 24 hours a day only on weekends. But in 1980, it became the first sports network to air 24 hours a day, 7 days a week!

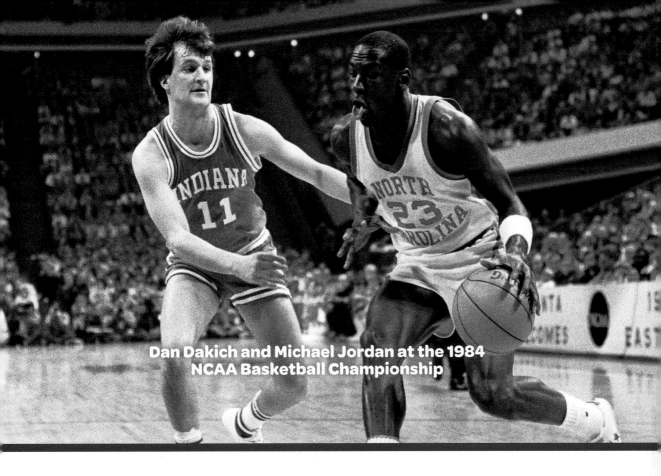

Dan Dakich and Michael Jordan at the 1984
NCAA Basketball Championship

In March 1980, ESPN began televising the early
rounds of the NCAA basketball **tournament**. This
became a popular event known as March Madness.
ESPN also wanted to air more professional sports. It
made a deal to air NBA basketball games in 1982. More
changes followed. A large television network called ABC
bought ESPN in 1984. Three years later, the NFL agreed
to let ESPN televise its football games. The games aired
on Sunday nights for 19 years. In 2006, ESPN began
airing games on Monday nights. Football fans loved
watching their favorite teams on ESPN. The network's
ratings soared!

Sealing the Victory

ESPN continued to grow through the 1980s and 1990s. It began to air professional hockey and baseball. This brought in many new viewers. The network continued airing lesser-known sports, too. The 1987 America's Cup sailing race gained national attention. People across the country loved cheering on the American team. By 1990, ESPN had become one of the top cable networks. Nearly 55 million people were **subscribed** to it.

1987 America's Cup

The Number One Sports Network

1980s-1990s tagline

First-Person View

ESPN introduced a tiny camera called the Crew Cam at a 1989 NASCAR race. It is mounted on a person's head. This allows the television audience to see whatever the wearer sees.

During this time, ESPN also expanded across the globe. The company formed ESPN **International** in 1988. Its purpose was to bring ESPN shows to viewers around the world. ESPN International launched networks such as ESPN Latin America and ESPN Asia. Today, ESPN has more than 32 networks in countries all over the globe. There are ESPN networks on all seven continents, including Antarctica!

The company soon expanded even more. It launched ESPN Radio in 1992. A television channel called ESPN2 soon followed. It was first aimed at a younger audience. The channel featured sports such as soccer and auto racing. The channel also covered extreme sports like **BMX** and snowboarding. In 1993, ESPN started the ESPY Awards. These awards honor top athletes, coaches, and teams. Many athletes have won an ESPY. Among them are Peyton Manning, LeBron James, and Serena Williams. In 2016, the Cleveland Cavaliers won the Best Team award!

All Sports, All the Time
1990s tagline

Serena Williams

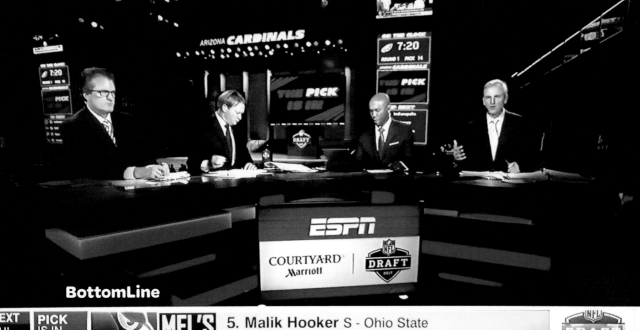

    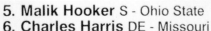

EXT
HI
ID

PICK IS IN		
RD1	13	#ARIpick

MEL'S
BEST AVAILABLE

5. Malik Hooker S - Ohio State
6. Charles Harris DE - Missouri

NFL DRAFT 2017

FL DRAFT | t DE/Texas A&M | 2 BEARS - Mitchell Trubisky QB/North Carolina | 3. 49ers - Sol

BottomLine

ESPN2 introduced the BottomLine in 1995. This black bar showed scores and sports news moving across the bottom of the television screen. It eventually became a feature of nearly every ESPN program. Over time, ESPN2 shifted its focus away from extreme sports and young viewers. The network is now aimed at viewers of all ages. It covers football, basketball, tennis, and many other popular sports.

....

Line It Up

ESPN introduced an electronic yellow line called "1st and Ten" in 1998. The line appears on the football field to television viewers. It shows how far a team needs to go to advance a ball.

Fired Up!

Today, nearly 90 million homes in the United States have ESPN. The network even airs sports played by kids! The Little League World Series is a popular event each summer. Fans can also see sports news and highlights on *SportsCenter*. This is one of ESPN's most popular shows. It gives up-to-the-minute news on games and athletes several times each day. More than 100 million people watch *SportsCenter* each month!

2002 Little League World Series

Many football fans look forward to watching *Monday Night Football* each week during the NFL season. They can also get daily football news and information on *NFL Live*. Another popular show is *30 for 30*. It features true stories about people and events in sports history. One episode covered Michael Jordan's basketball career. Another featured a famous racehorse named Haru Urara. *Outside the Lines* features stories about athletes and important issues they face. An episode about football players and brain injuries won a **Peabody Award**!

Popular ESPN Shows

Show	Launch Date
SportsCenter	1979
Baseball Tonight	1990
Outside the Lines	1990
Monday Night Countdown	1993
NFL Live	1998
Pardon the Interruption	2001
Around the Horn	2002
Monday Night Football	2006
First Take	2007
E:60	2007
SportsNation	2009
30 for 30	2009

Global Sports News

SportsCenter is one of ESPN's most popular shows. It is broadcast in eight different languages!

ESPN events draw many fans. The ESPN Wide World of Sports Complex hosts more than 200 sporting events each year. The complex is located at Walt Disney World in Florida. It has several sports **venues**. These include a baseball stadium, soccer fields, and tennis courts. Athletes of all ages and ability levels participate.

ESPN started the X Games in 1995. This event gives athletes the chance to compete in extreme sports. Many athletes perform exciting and sometimes dangerous tricks. The Summer X Games feature events such as skateboarding, motocross, and BMX. The Winter X Games test athletes' skills on snowboards, skis, and snowmobiles.

ESPN Wide World of Sports Complex

2010 X Games

ESPN also covers eSports, or electronic sports. These are organized multiplayer video game competitions. People play video games in front of large audiences. They compete for money and other prizes. **Drone** racing is also becoming popular with viewers. In these events, people race drones through obstacle courses. The drones can reach speeds up to 120 miles (193 kilometers) per hour!

Ryan Sheckler

Super Skater

In 2003, skateboarder Ryan Sheckler was the youngest person ever to win a gold medal at the X Games. He was 13.

17

A Team Player

ESPN helps people and their communities. The company gives money to organizations that support a variety of causes. One provides sports equipment to kids. Another helps kids of all abilities participate in sports together. ESPN donates to **food banks** across the United States. It also builds sports courts and fields in countries around the world.

ESPN also cares about the environment. The company promotes recycling on the job and at its events. Many ESPN employees **volunteer** in their communities. Some serve as coaches. Others pick up trash or plant trees.

Basketball coach Jim Valvano and ESPN started the V **Foundation** in 1993. It raises money to support cancer research. The My Wish program gives children the chance to meet their favorite athletes. ESPN inspires people of all ages to enjoy sports both as fans and as athletes!

True Sports Heroes

ESPN gives awards to athletes and teams who are making a positive difference in their communities. The San Francisco Giants won the award in 2016. They created a program that aims to end violence.

Johnny Cueto

a fan meeting athlete Tim Tebow
through the My Wish program

ESPN Timeline

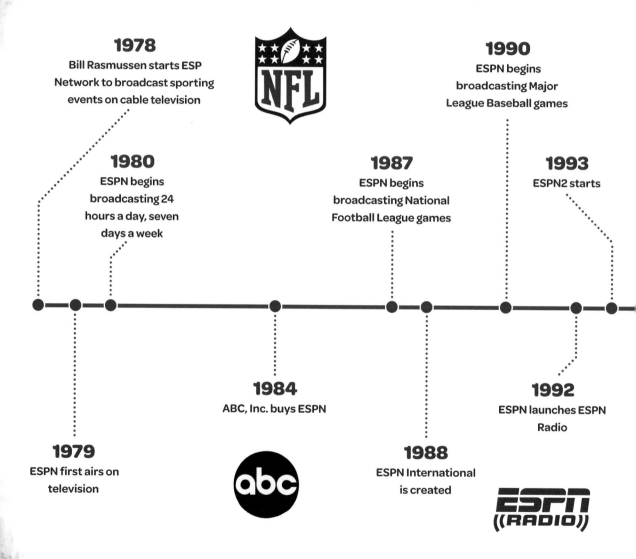

1978
Bill Rasmussen starts ESP
Network to broadcast sporting
events on cable television

1980
ESPN begins
broadcasting 24
hours a day, seven
days a week

1990
ESPN begins
broadcasting Major
League Baseball games

1987
ESPN begins
broadcasting National
Football League games

1993
ESPN2 starts

1984
ABC, Inc. buys ESPN

1992
ESPN launches ESPN
Radio

1979
ESPN first airs on
television

1988
ESPN International
is created

ESPN**HD**

1995
ESPN.com
launches

1998
ESPN The Magazine
is launched

2003
ESPN HD, a
high-definition
television sports
network, is
introduced

SPORTS CENTER

2013
ESPN's
SportsCenter
app launches

1997
Winter
X Games start

2009
EA Sports and ESPN
win an Emmy for the
EA Playbook

1995
X Games start in
Rhode Island

2011
The WatchESPN
app launches

1996
Walt Disney Company
becomes ESPN's
parent company

2009
ESPN builds a lab in Walt
Disney World's Wide
World of Sports to test
new gear and technology

Glossary

advertiser—a company that uses notices and messages to announce or promote something

apps—small, specialized programs downloaded onto smartphones and other mobile devices

BMX—bicycle motocross; in BMX, participants ride a bicycle on rough ground or over an obstacle course.

brand—a category of products all made by the same company

broadcasting—transmitting programs or information by radio or television

complex—a group of buildings or facilities that have a similar purpose

drone—a flying robot guided by a remote control

food banks—places that collect and store food for organizations that give it to people free of charge

foundation—an institution that provides funds to charitable organizations

headquarters—a company's main office

international—outside of the United States

logo—a symbol or design that identifies a brand or product

NCAA—the National Collegiate Athletic Association; the NCAA is an organization that oversees college sports.

networks—television companies that produce programs that people watch

Peabody Award—an award given to television and radio stations, websites, and other media for excellence in broadcasting

satellite—a piece of equipment that orbits around Earth

subscribed—paid money for a service

tournament—a sports competition with many players or teams that continues for several days or more

venues—places where events happen

volunteer—to do something for others without expecting money in return

To Learn More

AT THE LIBRARY

Cupp, Dave. *TV-Station Secrets*. Mankato, Minn.: Child's World, 2009.

Frederick, Shane. *The Kids' Guide to Sports Media*. North Mankato, Minn.: Capstone Press, 2014.

Teitelbaum, Michael. *Sports Broadcasting*. Ann Arbor, Mich.: Cherry Lake Publishing, 2009.

ON THE WEB

Learning more about ESPN is as easy as 1, 2, 3.

1. Go to www.factsurfer.com.

2. Enter "ESPN" into the search box.

3. Click the "Surf" button and you will see a list of related web sites.

With factsurfer.com, finding more information is just a click away.

Index